Watchwords

WATCHWORDS
ROGER
McGOUGH

Jonathan Cape Thirty Bedford Square London

First published 1969
© 1969 by Roger McGough

Jonathan Cape Ltd
30 Bedford Square, London WC1

SBN Paperback 224 61706 0
SBN Hardback 224 61705 2

'My Busseductress' and 'Soil' first appeared in *Twentieth Century*, 3rd issue, 1968.

Printed and bound in Great Britain
by Richard Clay (The Chaucer Press), Ltd
Bungay, Suffolk

Contents

Watchwords

watch the words
watch words the
watchword is
watch words are   away
sly as boots
ifyoutakeyoureyesoffthemforaminute

                              they're   up   and

                                                 allover

                                      the

                                                place

Assass   in

there is an assass
in the house
hold me tight
hold me tight
hold me and my shad
oh love will surely
find a way out
side a policeman
disguised as an owl
snuggles down in the old oak
not giving a hoot
and dreams of policewomen
disguised as mice

Kinetic poem no. 2

with love
give me your hand
some stranger
is fiction than truth

without love
I'm justa has
been away
too long in the tooth

My Busseductress

She is as beautiful as bustickets
and smells of old cash
drinks Guinness off duty
eats sausage and mash.
But like everyone else
she has her busdreams too
when the peakhour is over
and there's nothing to do.

A fourposter upstairs
a juke-box inside
there are more ways than one
of enjoying a ride.
Velvet curtains on the windows
thick carpets on the floor
roulette under the stairs
a bar by the door.

Three times a day
she'd perform a strip-tease
and during the applause
say nicely 'fares please'.
Upstairs she'd reserve
for men of her choice
invite them along
in her best Ribble voice.

She knows it sounds silly
what would the police say
but thinks we'd be happier
if she had her way.
There are so many youngmen

she'd like to know better
give herself with the change
if only they'd let her.

She is as beautiful as bustickets
and smells of old cash
drinks Guinness off duty
eats sausage and mash.
But she has her busdreams
hot and nervous
my blueserged queen
of the transport service.

The Hippopotamusman

Into the world of the red glass bus
came a man with a face like a hippopotamus

Grotesqueeruptions made horrific
an otherwise normal ugly face
Wartsscrambled over his head
peeping between thin twigs of dry hair
like pink shiny sunsets
Hanging below the neckline
like grapes festering on a vine
And when he blinked
you could glimpse the drunken dance
in the whites of his eyes
like the flash of underpants
through unbuttoned trouserflies

Had the passengers been in groups
there might have been laughter
But they were all singles
and turning their faces to the windows
did not see the view
but behind the privacy of eyelids
had a mental spew

Limpinggropingly looking for a place
went the substandard man
with the hunchbacked face
and finding one sat
and beholding his mudstudded boots
the hippopotamusman
wondered whether it was wednesday.

Hoarding

all too busy boarding

thirty year old numbskill
with a change of dirty coats
every single day gets porridge
but never gets his oats

all too busy boarding
the xmas merry-go-round

old lady sits by the firegrate
knitting a pudding with twine
dreams of brandy sauce
drinks methylated wine

all too busy boarding
the xmas merry-go-round
hoarding hoarding hoarding

girl in the secondhand nightie
with bruises on her brain
dips her thumb in the coldcream
sucks it over again

all too busy boarding
the xmas merry-go-round
hoarding hoarding hoarding
forgodssake   giveusapound

The Stranger

'Look quickly!' said the stranger
I turned around in time to see
a wall fall onto the child
playing beside a derelict house
In the silence of the rising dust
I saw the child's arm thrust
out stiff between the bricks
like a tulip
                        a white tulip
                                        a clenched tulip

I turned angrily to the stranger
'Why did you have to tell me?'
'Well I thought you'd want to see' he said
the tulip screamed
                        now limp
                                        now red

Soil

we've ignored eachother for a long time
and I'm strictly an indoor man
anytime to call would be the wrong time
I'll avoid you as long as I can

When I was a boy
We were good friends
I made pies out of you
When you were wet
And in childhood's glorious
Summer weather
We just roughandtumbled together
We were very close

just me and you and the sun
the world a place for having fun
always so much to be done

But gradually
I grew away from you
Of course you were still there
During my earliest sexcapades
When I roughandfumbled
Not very well after bedtime
But during my first pubescent winter
You seemed very wet and dirty
So I stayed indoors
And acquired a taste
For girls and clean clothes

we found less and less to say
you were jealous so one day
I simply upped and moved away

I still called to see you on occasions
But we had little now in common
And my visits grew less frequent
Until finally
One coldbright April morning
Many years ago
A handful of you
Drummed on my father's
Waxworked coffin

at last it all made sense
there was no need for pretence
you said nothing in defence

And now just recently
While travelling from town to town
Past where you live
I have suddenly become aware
Of you watching me out there
Quietly waiting
Playing patience with the trees

we've avoided eachother for a longtime
and I'm strictly a city man
anytime to call would be the wrong time
I'll avoid you as long as I can.

Snipers

When I was kneehigh to a tabletop,
Uncle Tom came home from Burma.
He was the youngest of seven brothers
so the street borrowed extra bunting
and whitewashed him a welcome.

All the relations made the pilgrimage,
including us, laughed, sang, made a fuss.
He was as brown as a chairleg,
drank tea out of a white mug the size of my head,
and said next to nowt.

But every few minutes he would scan
the ceiling nervously, hands begin to shake.
'For snipers,' everyone later agreed,
'A difficult habit to break.'

Sometimes when the two of us were alone,
he'd have a snooze after dinner
and I'd keep an eye open for Japs.
Of course, he didn't know this
and the tanner he'd give me before I went
was for keeping quiet,
but I liked to think it was money well spent.

Being Uncle Tom's secret bodyguard
had it's advantages, the pay was good
and the hours were short, but even so,
the novelty soon wore off, and instead,
I started school and became an infant.

B   17

Later, I learned that he was in a mental home.
'Needn't tell anybody ... Nothing serious
... Delayed shock ... Usual sort of thing
... Completely cured now the doctors say.'
The snipers came down from the ceiling
but they didn't go away.

Over the next five years they picked off
three of his brothers; one of whom was my father.
No glory, no citations,
Bang! straight through the heart.

Uncle Tom's married now, with a family.
He doesn't say much, but each night after tea,
he still dozes fitfully in his favourite armchair,
(dreams by courtesy of Henri Rousseau).
He keeps out of the sun, and listens now and then
for the tramp tramp tramp of the Colonel Bogeymen.
He knows damn well he's still at war,
just that the snipers aren't Japs anymore.

snowscene

snow crackles underfoot
like powdered bones
trees have dandruff
in their hair
and the wind moans
    the wind moans

ponds are wearingglasses
with lenses three feet deep
birds are silent in the air
as stones
and the wind can't sleep
    the wind can't sleep

i found an oldman by the road
who had not long been dead
i had not heard his lonely groans
nor seen him weep
only birds heard the last words he said
before the wind pulled a sheet o'er his head
    the wind pulled a sheet o'er his head

'The Fight of the year'

'And there goes the bell for the third month
and Winter comes out of its corner looking groggy
Spring leads with a left to the head
followed by a sharp right to the body
    daffodils
    primroses
    crocuses
    snowdrops
    lilacs
    violets
    pussywillow
Winter can't take much more punishment
and Spring shows no signs of tiring
    tadpoles
    squirrels
    baalambs
    badgers
    bunny rabbits
    mad march hares
    horses and hounds
Spring is merciless
Winter won't go the full twelve rounds
    bobtail clouds
    scallywaggy winds
    the sun
    a pavement artist
    in every town
A left to the chin
and Winter's down!
  1 tomatoes
  2 radish
  3 cucumber

4   onions
5   beetroot
6   celery
7   and any
8   amount
9   of lettuce
10 for dinner
Winter's out for the count
Spring is the winner!'

poem about the sun slinking off and pinning up a notice

the sun
hasn't got me fooled
not for a minute
just when
you're beginning to believe
that   grass is green
and   skies are blue
and   colour is king
hey   ding a ding ding
and

      a

          host

              of

                    other

                           golden

                                  etceteras

before you know where you are
he's slunk off somewhere
and pinned up a notice saying:

      MOON

If I were Poet Laureate

If I were Poet Laureate
purveyor of words to the Queen
I'd make some welcome changes
and liven up the scene

I'd wear silver lamé trousers
and a velvet jacket of black
with 'By Royal Appointment'
in gold letters on me back

I'd be on Television
twenty-four hours a day
shouting 'Death to Politicians'
(in a nice sort of way)

And with me fiery verses
I'd upset the applecart
and cause a revolution
for a giggle just for a start

I'd move into the Houses of Parliament
gerrin a couple of crates
a lorryload of dollies
and invite me poetry mates

I'd scatter the existing cabinet
to the wind like so much chaff
and fill it with comedians
at least we'd have a laugh

As Chancellor of the Exchequer
Ken Dodd should do the trick

get rid of all the taxes
with a wave of his tickling stick

Milligan in the Foreign Office
Secombe in the Treasury
Morecambe Minister of Transport
with Wise thrown in for good measury

And once things were shaping
I suppose I really ought
invite Kenneth Williams
to be Minister of Sport

If people thought me loony
I'd prove I could be loonier
hand over the Ministry of Arts
to Hubert Selby Junior

Monkhouse Cooper Askey
Yarwood Tarbuck Ray
could all take turns apiece
playing Prime Minister for a day

If I were Poet Laureate
wordsmith to the Queen
I'd make our little country
the swingiest place you'd seen

And her majesty would send for me
and I would go to greet her
bring a smile to her gracious face
in me own inimitable metre

Oh if I were Poet Laureate
I'd never eat me words
you'd get muck like this
and I'd get all the birds.

My little plastic mac

Teach me, o Lord, to be permissive
the 'sixties way to save the soul
three leers for sexual freedom
let the good times rock'nroll.

Tired of being puritan
and living by the code
I learned the New Morality
and shed my guilty load.

I read the kinky magazines
to gain my evil ends
scanned the personal columns
for interesting friends.

And now I've got the taste for sin
I know I'll never stop
just can't wait to get married
so I'll have a wife to swap.

Edna O'Brien is my pin-up girl
every book of hers I've read
and I've got a photo of Brigid Brophy
on the wall above my bed.

But Penny Mortimer is my favourite
I think she's awful nice
and often when I'm troubled
I write to her for advice.

She acknowledged my first inquiry
but now she never replies
but the thought of being her co-respondent
brings a tear to my eyes.

I'm all for divorce and abortion
and the contraceptive pill
so three rousing queers from the audience
for the homosexual bill.

Here's to the New Morality
pornographers may they thrive
when there's blue films on at the Odeon
it'll be good to be alive.

And once the ball starts rolling
who knows very soon
there'll be a complete set of the Marquis de Sade
in every hotel room.

God bless the new reformers
let them make our island home
a country fit for psychopaths
and nutters like me to roam.

You see at bedtime when I've put away
my flagellation kit
I often shed a silent tear
and I'm forced to admit
that it isn't always easy
being a sexual maniac
as I slide between the rubber sheets
in my little plastic mac.

Knees down Mother Brown

This story really started
back in 1963
when I passed my exams
for university

I was very working class
in those early days
but three years up at Oxford
made me change my ways

So if you'd care to listen
I'll tell you if I may
how tragedy befell me
on graduation day

Everyone assembled
in the Convocation Hall
students and their parents
gents and ladies all

Nervously I waited
in mortar-board and gown
for the Dean to call my name
'Next student Charlie Brown'

When suddenly from the back
there came a drunken shout
and thro' the door came mum and dad
with a crate of stout

Then a coachload of relations
staggered into view
singing 'Charlie Brown in Liverpool
we're really proud of you'

Professors Lords and Ladies
really looked askance
when mother clambered on the stage
and there began to dance

Knees down Mother Brown
Knees down Mother Brown
I'm at Oxford now you know
ee aye ee aye addio

Knees down Mother Brown
Knees down Mother Brown
Look at the state o'
My old mater
Knees down Mother Brown

A student shouted angrily
'We want our degrees
not a drunken lady's
fat and hairy knees'

On hearing this I leapt up
and gave the chap a clout
'Watch it lar that's my mar
you're talking about'

Soon everyone was fighting
pandemonium broke out
but unperturbed Mother Brown
gaily danced throughout

Knees down Mother Brown
Knees down Mother Brown
Dearie Dearie Dearie me
Now I won't get my degree

Knees down Mother Brown
Knees down Mother Brown
Look at the state o'
My old mater
Knees down Mother Brown

The assembly hall next morning
was in a sorry state
and I need hardly tell you
I didn't graduate

And now I'm on the old King Cole
back in Liverpool town
just because my mother
couldn't keep them down

Knees down Mother Brown
Knees down Mother Brown
Need you be so working class
get up Mother off your——

Knees down Mother Brown
Knees down Mother Brown
Look at the state o'
My old mater
Knees down Mother Brown

Poem for the opening of Christ The King Cathedral, Liverpool

O Lord on thy new Liverpool address
let no bombs fall
Gather not relics in the attic
nor dust in the hall
But daily may a thousand friends
who want to chat just call

Let it not be a showroom
for wouldbe good Catholics
or worse:
a museum
a shrine
a concrete hearse
But let it be a place
Where lovers meet after work
for kind words and kisses
Where dockers go of a Saturday night
to get away from the missus
Tramps let kip there through till morning
kids let rip there every evening

Let us pray there
heads held high
arms to the sky
not afraid and kneeling
let Koppites
teach us how to sing
God's 'Top of the Pops' with feeling

After visiting you
May trafficwardens let noisy parkers off
and policemen dance on the beat

Barrowomen knock a shilling off
exatheists sing in the street

And let the cathedral laugh
Even show its teeth
And if it must wear the cassock of dignity
Then let's glimpse the jeans beneath

O Lord on thy new Liverpool address
let no bombs fall
Keep always a light in the window
a welcome mat in the hall
That it may be a home sweet
home from home for all.

Funland

Once upon a time there was a country called
England. Now the English, as they were
affectionately known, were a fun-loving race, who
prided themselves on their mini-skirts, their
popgroups, their bingo-callers, their footballers.
It was a nation steeped in tradition and quicksand.
It was the swingiest, sexiest, most bubblesome
place on earth.

        But like every inflationary trend
        All good swings come to an end.

The bubble burst. In the midst of the party, the
drink ran out and the Prime Minister bankruptured
himself.

        So eating humble pie
        He prayed to God on high.

And God, who at the time was disguised as a French
General, blew on his nose to summon a meeting of the
world leaders.

        And all the powers met
        England's future to decide
        While Harold, pipe in hand,
        Stood in the rain outside.

And for weeks they talked
and Harold got wetter
and his pipe warped. Until eventually they
decided that for needless frivolity in the face

of impending disaster, England should be punished
by being forced to supply the world with its most
saleable commodity – Fun.

>So they pooled their resources
>To build a gigantic fair
>Covering the whole of England
>Solving unemployment there.

>They built a plastic dome
>From the Channel to the Clyde
>Designed a nuclear sun
>And hung it up inside.

They called it Funland, and every man
woman and child over the age of five,
in overalls designed by Hardy Amies,
was forced to work on the helter-skelters, the
ghost-trains, the big wheels, the dodgems,
the ice-cream stalls.

>Hot dogs and Englishmen
>Out in the nuclear sun
>Sweating at the engines
>For foreigners to have fun.

There is a place called Funland
To the north of Germany
And many many years ago
They say it used to be
A country called England
And that apparently
The sad-eyed clowns who work there
Once had all been free.

The Russian Bear

The Russian Bear itself must save
from its self-inflicted plight
Having hollowed out the darkest cave
complains there is no light.

The Russian Bear is angry
snarls and stamps around
Clawing at the echoes
from the underground.

Smarting with the lovebites
blindly now the bear
Curses its inheritance
and pulls out its fur.

So to labour camps the culprits go
not afraid to cry
Tracing poems in the snow
in letters seven years high.

But one day
Yevtushenko will stand on the bridge at midnight
throwing Sputniks at the moon
As a Commissar in Lennongrad eats his speeches with a spoon.
The K.G.B. will be replaced by the W.V.S.
and Nureyev will admit that its all a load of Bolshoi.
They will raise the school-leaving age to thirty-two
And Zhivago will again meet Lara, kiss
and handinhand walk into the sunset
Across the vast expanse of the pillow.

34

So to all graphomaniacs of Greece, Rhodesia, Czechoslovakia
and other tonguetwisted nations
Who scribble after curfew
and keep ideals under the floorboards
with the grenades;
A message of hope from
Galanskov, Ginzburg, Dobrovolsky, Lashnova, Litvinov,
'If the heart bleeds love, bare it,
If the martyr's crown fits, wear it.'

10.15 thursday morning Memphis Tennessee

10.15 thursday morning
Memphis Tennessee

Another martyr for old glory
Another murder for the crowd
Luther King he died for freedom
Freedom really did him proud

And then just two months later
Forgive but not forget
One more psychossassination
Another hero gone and yet ... ...

How time flies when you teach it how to fly
A fading black speck in a newly whitewashed sky

Everywhere Mister Death breathes
                      death breathes

violence breeds
violence breeds
violence breeds
violence breeds
          violence
every   where there's a will
                            there's a way   of life
                            is for living   is for living
All the world over   everyone is the same
integration   is the name of the game
integration spelt   L O V E

L O V E spells

love is the distance between freedom and the fighter
measured in chains

love is the distance between the soldier and the politician
measured in halfmasts

love is the distance between Alabama and Johannesburg
measured in goosesteps

love is the distance between slavery and equality
measured in education, in poems, songs, tears and laughter

Evil is all around   there's a lesson to learn
Pour paraffin on your love
Put a match to your heart
let it BURN BABY BURN

AND YOU KNOW? THE DIFFERENCE BETWEEN BLACK
   POWER AND WHITE POWER
IS THAT BLACK POWER IS A *WHITE* CRUCIFIX AGAINST
   A *BLACK* SKY

AND THE DIFFERENCE BETWEEN SOMEONE WHO LOVES
AND SOMEONE WHO HATES
IS THAT SOMEONE WHO HATES HAS TO EXPLAIN WHAT
   HE MEANS

                                        the means
                                        justify the end
                        the end   less waiting for God
                        oh Lord
Give us a sign oh Lord,   Give us auld lang syne oh Lord

         so onward gentle soldiers
         hear the bugler call
         let's all march together
         or let's not march at all

and now hold hands
we'll show 'em
black words
white paper
a poem

When the Epilogue's over

When the Epilogue's over and transmission closed down
Television sets switched off all over town
And viewers gone upstairs to tune in to their dreams
When cameras are garaged for the night
The building emptied and out goes the light
Then everything isn't what it seems

For the studios in the twinkling of an eye
Are haunted by programmes of days long gone by
'What's My Line' 'Face to Face' 'Compact'
'Quatermass' 'Six-Five Special' 'T.W.3'
The hits of yesterday like old soldiers never die
They're only stored away

Richard Dimbleby is Controller of Programmes
With Gilbert Harding as his right-hand man
And although their work is mainly administrative
They appear whenever they can
Handley Hancock Arthur Haynes
Frinton Flanagan Jimmy James
Provide the phantom fun and games
Randall Wilton Miller
Oliver Formby Hay
All sing a song or simply 'I say I say I say'
Some nights Harry Lauder Dan Leno Marie Lloyd
And other stars of the Music Hall
Try out their act on B.B.C.
And they're not too bad at all

And so it goes on through the night and everynight
An eternity of sameold gags and songs
Until dawn clocks in with a hangover

And as a thousand commissionaires
Assemble for morning prayers
And a bevy of chars in chauffeurdriven cars
Arrive at the Centre
Silver-topped mops ready to use
Before cameras manned by skeleton crews
A dead announcer reads yesterdays news

Sundeath/greentears

when you said you loved me
the sun
leapt out from behind st georges hall
and ran around town;
       kissing younggirls' faces
       exposing fatmen's braces
       freeing birds & chasing flies
       pulling hats down over eyes
       making bobbies get undressed
       barrowladies look their best
       wayside winos sit and dream
       hotdogmen to sell ice-cream

but when you said goodbye
i heard that the sun
had been runover
somewhere in castle street
by a busload of lovers
whom you have yet to meet

Man the Barricades, the Enemy has let loose his Pyjamas!

yesterday
secure behind
your barricade
of polite coffeecups
you sat
whittling clichés

but lastnight
slyold me
got you up
some dark alleyway
of my dreams

this morning
you have a   **faraway look**
in your
smalltalk

Poem on being in love with two girls at the same time

i have a photograph of you
in the insidepocket of my head
        a blurrred photograph
        a double image
is it one girl or is it two?
is it her or is it you?
            Damcamara
            Damcamara

Poppoem

You're as bored as butterscotch
it's obvious we're through
silkstockings lying on the chair
sunshine sticks like glue
Kids are playing warriors
in the blancoed yard outside
I tried to think of something
I tried,   I tried,   I tried.

The cat sleeps on the lino
dreaming of frozen mice
you stroke your thigh with a hairbrush back
pretending that it's ice
A warrior triumphant
takes a dustbin for a ride
crying 'Fear no more the tyrant
He died,   he died   he died.'

The clock complains of sunstroke
and then is heard no more
a sick violin is put to bed
by the corporal next door
The lid slips off the dustbin
the warrior falls inside
spreadeagled hurt his bottom
and his pride,   his pride,   his pride.

You throw the hairbrush at the cat
and walk toward the door
trace a final farewell
in footprints on the floor
I thought about the violin
and of the clock that died
and like the wounded warrior
I cried,   I cried,   I cried.

44

Who Was The Naughty Girl

Who was the naughty girl i saw
making love with a bluebell,
who was the naughty girl i saw
paying her fare with a seashell
who was the naughty girl i saw
sawing the seasaw in two
Who reported Dr Barnardo to the N.S.P.C.C.
Who reported Peter Scott to the R.S.P.C.A.
Who sent Dr Ramsey a Playboy key
Jack Ruby a getwell card
Dr Crippen a Valentine card
The Boston strangler a calling card
Pontius Pilate a Xmas card
Who passed Lot the salt
Who went to lunch with Bill Burroughs, naked
Who fed foie gras to the geese
Who helped the blindman into the ladies
Who snitched on Guy Fawkes
Who switched on Caryl Chessman
Who knitted socks for Viet Cong
Who thought L.B.J. was a lemon drink
Who thought the port of Liverpool was V.P.
Who married a Pakistani, bought a house in Coronation Street
and closed the series
Who thought Powellism was the Boy Scout movement
Who crossed a prostitute with an orang utang & produced
one who swung from lamp-post to lamp-post and did it for
peanuts
Who put L.S.D. in my Horlicks
Evostick in my contact lenses
chloroform in my handkerchief
pig's eggs in my pockets

ants in my gants
Who was the naughty girl?
Why
YOU

S.W.A.L.K.

There's a littlegirl called Laetitia
and she writes the most amazing letters
to the poets & the singers
anyone whose on the scene
in bold italic script
she makes suggestions most outrageous
she's got six G.C.E.s
and she's only just fifteen

To the north of Wolverhampton
in a facsimile semi
when the homework has been put away
and so has her tea
in the silence of her bedroom
she makes pen & ink advances
the undisputed teenage queen
of pop pornography

Spinning stuff wet dreams are made of
on lilaccoloured paper
in envelopes marked 'personal'
Sealed With A Loving Kiss
she puts a bundle in her satchel
for breaktime pillarboxing
then goes downstairs for Ovaltine
a ritualistic miss

All the poets & the singers
impatient for the postman
eat cornflakes with eggspoons
& loiter near the door
their wives note the excitement

as one letter is secreted
assume it's from a lover
CRY HAVOC and let loose the t-a-r-a-n-t-u-l-a-s of war

There's a littlegirl called Laetitia
and she writes the most amazing letters
to the cardboard cutout heroes
of pubescent fantasy
inviting rape by proxy
a carnal correspondent
she's the undisputed teenage queen
of pop pornography.

Discretion

Discretion is the better part of Valerie
though all of her is nice
lips as warm as strawberries
eyes as cold as ice
the very best of everything
only will suffice
not for her potatoes
and puddings made of rice

Not for her potatoes
and puddings made of rice
she takes carbohydrates
like God takes advice
a surfeit of ambition
is her particular vice
Valerie fondles lovers
like a mousetrap fondles mice

And though in the morning
she may whisper : 'it was nice'
you can tell by her demeanour
that she keeps her love on ice
but you've lost your hardearned heart
now you'll have to pay the price
for she'll kiss you on the memory
and vanish in a trice

Valerie is corruptible
but known to be discreet
Valerie rides a silver cloud
where once she walked the street.

49

My cat and i

Girls are simply the prettiest things
My cat and i believe
And we're always saddened
When it's time for them to leave

We watch them titivating
(that often takes a while)
And though they keep us waiting
My cat & i just smile

We like to see them to the door
Say how sad it couldn't last
Then my cat and i go back inside
And talk about the past.

The Act of Love

The Act of Love lies somewhere
between the belly and the mind
I lost the love sometime ago
Now I've only the act to grind.

Brought her home from a party
don't bother swapping names
identity's not needed
when you're only playing games.

High on bedroom darkness
we endure the pantomime
ships that go bang in the night
run aground on the sands of time.

Saved in the nick of dawn
its cornflakes and then goodbye
another notch on the headboard
another day wondering why.

The Act of Love lies somewhere
between the belly and the mind
I lost the love sometime ago
Now I've only the act to grind.

Orgasm

(Paroxysm of desire, or rage or other passion – The Pocket
Oxford English Dictionary)

Just a boy soprano in a gilded choir
racked with religion guilt and desire
like magazines for men hidden under the shelf
sex was a secret I kept to myself
summer was boring
but winter was fine
when a girl first chanced on an orgasm of mine

My secret a secret now everyone shared
'Treason' I cried 'no girl shall be spared'
with goldlamé armour and velvetine sword
a pagan crusader through bedrooms I roared
schooldays were brutal
but evenings were fine
when virgins were lanced on orgasms of mine

When the war had ended I gathered the spoils
learned the guitar and painted in oils
I dressed to thrill and I danced to impress
invented conundrums and drank to excess
mornings were hungover
but the nights they were fine
when youngladies danced on orgasms of mine

And one in particular seemed better than most
as she skipped and she tripped from pillow to post
she stayed for the encores and of course very soon
seduced the whole orchestra and called the tune
oh the takings were good
but the giving divine
for now the orgasms were not only mine

But sadly the bride came before the fall
I'd settled for one though I'd wanted them all
now i reek of nostalgia and aftershave lotions
as i conjure the past and i go through the motions
on the stable door
there hangs now a sign:
'Who'll swap an orgasm for one of mine?'

Bachelor of Love

Ten years old and the Engelbert Humperdinck
of Star of the Sea County Primary
Learning to read and write time I had of it
Free milk and the cane to keep me warm
When I danced by the light
of a barrage balloon
then hand in handed home
with the love-locked ankle-socked
star of Junior 3

And then the years of the long grass
when education became secondary
and armed to the teeth for sin
I kept my books in a leather pillowcase
And went to school
in a doublebreasted gaberdine eiderdown

At university made the grade
learned every trick of the trade
Never missed out on a chance
at a party or a dance
Knew flattery could hypnotize
gave little presents wrapped in lies
A lightfingered lethal Lord of the Flies

Learned feminine secrets in one fell snoop
whispered suggestions
then let out a hoop
I was the ego
I gathered wallflowers
goo goo goo chook

But hear the hunchbacked prisoner say
'Believe me Time doesn't pay'
One day the hourglass cracked
The citadel of my heart was sacked

I fell in love
Lived in a dream
(you know the sort of thing I mean)
*

But she was a feminine version of me
passed the audition and landed the part
And I saw what I hadn't paid to see
when I peeped through the keyhole of her heart

someone's fingers in her hair someone's jodhpurs on my chair

So beware all ye who choose to flirt
lest someone poisons your just dessert
As the weal of fate reveals
Time wounds all heels

But life goes on
and I occasionally take my pleasure
Sellotape on the hourglass
(a temporary measure)
But life goes on
and I'll remember all I've learned then take a deep breath
When I tumble into bed with Mistress Death

i see a heartshaped wreath
on a wooden cross nailed
and inscribed underneath
'Here lies McGough, B.A. Love (failed)'

> * Here twelve stanzas I've left out
> (in case she reads this) about
> the sad, the happy times,
> how we lived between the rhymes.

If life's a lousy picture, why not leave before the end

Don't worry
one night we'll find that deserted kinema
the torches extinguished
the cornish ripples locked away in the safe
the tornoff tickets chucked
in the tornoff shotbin
the projectionist gone home to his nightmare

Don't worry
that film will still be running
(the one about the sunset)
& we'll find two horses
tethered in the front stalls
& we'll mount
& we'll ride off
        into
            our
               happy
                  ending